Exploring
Seeds

by Kristin Sterling

first step nonfiction

Lerner Publications Company · Minneapolis

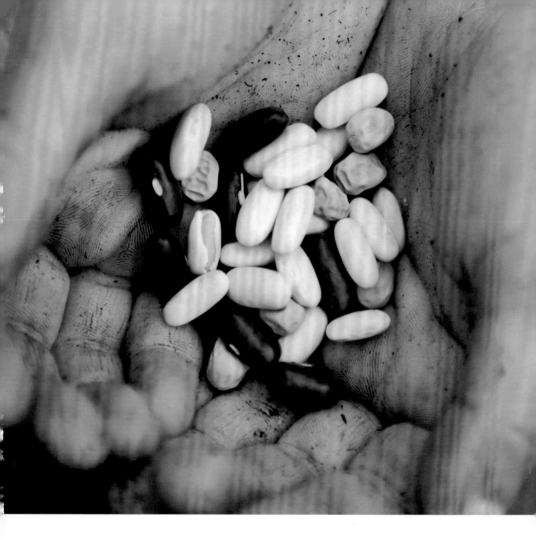

I see **seeds**.

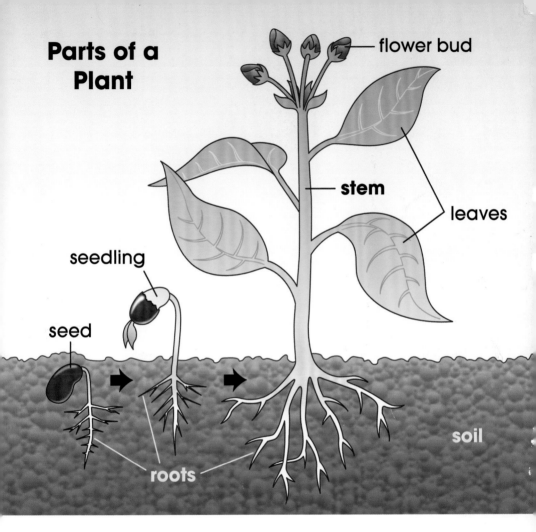

Parts of a Plant

flower bud

stem

leaves

seedling

seed

roots

soil

Seeds are parts of plants.

3

Each seed can become a
new plant.

Seeds need water and soil to grow.

Seeds crack open in the
ground. They send roots
down into the soil.

Stems from the seeds go up
into the sunlight.

Soon leaves and flowers
grow.

Foods we eat form around
the flowers and the leaves.

People plant seeds on farms
and in gardens.

Seeds are also blown by
wind and moved by water.

Seeds grow in pinecones.

Plums have large seeds
inside called pits.

13

People can eat seeds!
Sunflower seeds are good
14 snacks.

You can eat the yellow
seeds of a corn plant.

Seeds are on your plate, in the ground, and all around 16 you.

Do you see seeds?

How Seeds Move

Seeds move in many ways. The seeds of coconuts float on water. The seeds of maple trees have wings. Wind spreads these seeds. Burrs are seed holders. They stick to animal fur. When the animal travels, so do the burrs. Chestnuts can travel this way. Nuts and berries are eaten by animals. The seeds are left behind in animal droppings.

coconut swimmers

maple tree fliers

chestnut stickers

nut treats

19

Seed Facts

 Poppy seeds are used in muffins. They are small, tasty seeds.

 Many people roast pumpkin seeds and eat them in the fall.

 Strawberries have seeds on the outside of the fruit.

 The outer layer of a seed is called a seed coat. Seed coats can be thin or thick.

Some seeds are not safe to eat. The seeds of a lily-of-the-valley plant can change how fast your heart beats.

 Some seeds stay in the ground for a long time. They need the right amount of water, warmth, and sunlight to sprout. Scientists found a seed that sprouted after 2,000 years!

Glossary

 roots – the parts of a plant that bring in water and keep a plant in the ground

 seeds – the plant parts that can make new plants

 soil – the dirt in which plants grow

 stem – the part of a plant that holds up the plant

Index

flower – 3, 8–9

leaves – 3, 8–9

pits – 13

roots – 3, 6

soil – 3, 5–6

stem – 3, 7

water – 5, 11

The images in this book are used with the permission of: © Rachel Weill/FoodPix/Getty Images, pp. 2, 22 (2nd from top); © Laura Westlund/Independent Picture Service, p. 3; © John Lund/Digital Vision/Getty Images, p. 4; © Will Heap/Getty Images, pp. 5, 22 (3rd from top); © Nigel Cattlin/Visuals Unlimited, Inc., pp. 6, 22 (1st from top); © Bogdan Wańkowicz/Dreamstime.com, pp. 7, 22 (bottom); © Weir2010/Dreamstime.com, p. 8; © Aleksandar Zoric/Dreamstime.com, p. 9; © Alistair Berg/Getty Images, p. 10; © blickwinkel/Alamy, p. 11; © Brent Hathaway/Dreamstime.com, p. 12; © Michael Rosenfeld/Photographer's Choice/Getty Images, p. 13; © Andersen Ross/Digital Vision/Getty Images, p. 14; © JGI/Jamie Grill/Belnd Images/Getty Images, p. 15; © Noam Armonn/Dreamstime.com, p. 16; © Ryan Beiler/Dreamstime.com, p. 17; © Inga Spence/Photo Researchers, Inc., p. 19 (top left); © Alessandrozocc/Dreamstime.com, p. 19 (top right); © Jin Yamada/Dreamstime.com, p. 19 (bottom left); © Elena Ryshkova/Dreamstime.com, p. 19 (bottom right).
Front cover: © Kaleff/Dreamstime.com

Main body text set in ITC Avant Garde Gothic 21/25. Typeface provided by Adobe Systems.

Lerner Publications Company
A division of Lerner Publishing Group, Inc.
241 First Avenue North
Minneapolis, MN 55401 U.S.A.

Website address: www.lernerbooks.com

Library of Congress Cataloging-in-Publication Data

Sterling, Kristin.
    Exploring seeds / by Kristin Sterling.
        p.   cm. — (First step nonfiction—Let's look at plants)
    Includes index.v
    ISBN 978-0-7613-5782-7 (lib. bdg. : alk. paper)
    1. Seeds—Juvenile literature. 2. Plant anatomy—Juvenile literature. I. Title . II. Series:
First step nonfiction. Plant parts.
QK661.S74 2012
581.4'67—dc22   2010042990

Manufactured in the United States of America
1 – PC – 7/15/11